WHEN LOVE FIRST FOUND ME

POETRIES OF A LOVE AWAKENING

AFSHA TABREZ MAHNOOR

Made with ♥ on the Notion Press Platform
www.notionpress.com

To the hearts that have loved, lost, and dared to love again.

To the silent readers who've felt the loudest emotions.

To those who find pieces of themselves between lines and verses.

This is for you—

for every tear shed, every smile shared,

and every moment that love made you feel alive.

May these words be a home for your heart.

Contents

Contents

Contents

Preface

Love has a way of finding us when we least expect it—softly, quietly, like the first touch of dawn on a sleepless tender night. It's tender and full of promises, and in its wake, it leaves stories worth telling. This collection began in those moments, when love found me for the first time and changed everything.

The poems in this book are pieces of my heart—raw, unfiltered, and true. They trace a journey many of us know but experience in our own ways: the euphoria of first love, the comfort of feeling seen, and the ache of realizing even love can falter. I wanted to capture it all—the beginning, the bloom, and the heartbreak that turned into healing.

This is not just my story. It's the story of anyone who has ever loved deeply and dared to let someone in. It's for those who believe in love, even when it hurts, and for those who carry the memories of it like a scar they have come to cherish.

From the first spark to final goodbye, these words are for you.

May you find a piece of your own heart in these pages.

Prologue

Poetry has always been my way of speaking when the heart cannot find its voice. In the quiet moments when words feel too heavy, too loud, or simply too much, I've turned to the language of verse to untangle the feelings i hold within. This book is the result of those quiet, sometimes painful, moments—the ones that make us question, grow, and ultimately transform.

When Love First Found Me began as a spark, a glimpse of something beautiful, something soft and fleeting. It was a whisper from the universe, the beginning of a story where love felt like a sunrise—warm, hopeful, and full of promise. But as the story unraveled, so did the truth that love is not only joy; it is also pain, longing, loss, and healing. The journey from first love to first heartbreak is not a straight line. It's filled with detours, pauses, and moments when you wonder if the end is the same as the beginning.

I offer it you, the reader, as a piece of my soul—a mirror of what feels like to be human, to love, and to survive the aftermath.

PART I

1. The Moment You Became Love

I never knew love had a face, Until I saw yours, a quiet grace.
A glance, a spark, a fleeting stare,
Suddenly, my world was there.
My heart once still, began to race,
A flutter, a tremor I couldn't trace.
In that moment, without a sound, i felt love rise from deep unbound
The way your eyes caught the light, Made everything feel soft, so bright.
I wondered if you knew it too—
That something had changed, and it was you.
No words were needed, no gentle sigh,
Just the knowing glance, the unspoken why.
I felt the warmth of your silent call, and realised I'd given my heart to it all.
For in that look, so shy, so pure,
I found a love I'm certain will endure.
It was you, It was us, though we hadn't begun—
Love came alive when our eyes met, one.

2. Before You Leave

The first time I saw you, my heart didn't know,
What it was, or where it would go.
A glance, a spark, and something new,
A feeling I couldn't yet see through.

But now, as you stand to leave,
I feel my heart begin to grieve.
The distance growing, the space between,
A quiet ache where love's been seen.

I never thought this would be the cost,
Of feeling something—of love now lost.
You're walking away, and I'm standing still,
A thousand words, but none to spill.

How do I hold this love inside,
When you're leaving, and I can't hide
The way my heart races, the way it yearns,
For a love that in silence, still burns.

I want to say more, but fear holds me tight,

So I watch you go, fading from sight.
And though I know it's just goodbye for now,
A piece of my heart stays with you somehow.
I'll wait, though time may steal the days,
For love first felt never fades away.
And maybe, when you return again,
My heart..
will feel the same as then

3. When I Saw You Again

The moment I saw you, my heart skipped a beat,
A rush of warmth, a pulse so sweet.
The world around me began to blur,
As my breath caught in a trembling stir.

Your gaze met mine, and time stood still,
A silent storm, a sudden thrill.
My heartbeat loud, a rhythmic plea,
Each thump a confession, silently.

I tried to speak, but the words wouldn't come,
For you were the rhythm, and I was undone.
In that fleeting moment, I knew it was true—
That something inside was waking anew.

The distance between us, it seemed so far,
Yet every step closer felt like a spark.
My pulse echoed with a truth untold,
A feeling I couldn't yet unfold.

In the quiet of your presence, I found my way,
My heart racing, as if to say—

I've missed you more than words can show,
And with you, my love continues to grow.

4. Forty-Six Minutes Of Us

The phone rang, and my heart took flight,
A voice I'd longed for lit up the night.
Forty-six minutes and forty-five,
Every second made me feel alive.

Your laughter danced like a gentle breeze,
Words so natural, they put me at ease.
No script, no plan, just you and me,
Talking like waves returning to the sea.

Your voice, a melody I'd never heard,
Carrying warmth in every word.
The world grew quiet, it faded away,
While I held on to everything you'd say.

I didn't want the moment to end,
This call felt more than just a friend.
Time passed, but it wasn't enough,
Hanging up was suddenly tough.

Now the silence hums, but I still smile,
Holding those moments for a while.
Forty-six minutes, a start so true,
And I can't wait to talk again with you.

5. Caught In The Flash

I tried to be quiet, so sly, so small,
To capture your face, the moment, it all.
My phone in my hand, I aimed with care,
But oh, the flashlight—bright and unfair!

It lit up the room, as clear as day,
And I froze, unsure what to say.
You turned to me, a laugh in your eyes,
Caught in my act, I couldn't disguise.

My cheeks burned red, my cover was blown,
I laughed too hard to feel alone.
"Just one quick photo," I tried to explain,
But your smile was worth all the playful pain.

Next time, I'll ask, no secrets to hide,
But I'll always remember the laugh we shared that night.

6. A Secret Crush

Each day and night, we talked so long,
Sharing stories, sweet and strong.
Your voice, a tune I'd always keep,
Even in dreams, even in sleep.

I held a secret, close to my heart,
Unsure of how or where to start.
So I told you, with careful tone,
"I have a crush, but it's unknown."

You asked me who, I laughed instead,
Hiding the truth, my cheeks turned red.
How could I say it? Would it feel right,
To tell you it's you I think of each night?

The words stayed silent, I couldn't reveal,
The depth of the love I wanted to feel.
But in that moment, my heart still knew,
Every word I said was meant for you.

7. When Dreams Spoke The Truth

Last night I dreamed, so soft, so clear,
Your voice was calm, your smile near.
You looked at me with knowing eyes,
As if my heart held no disguise.

You said, "I know, you don't have to hide,
The way you feel, it's in your eyes."
I froze in place, my breath held tight,
But your words felt warm, not full of fright.

You smiled and said, "It's always been you,
I've felt it too, though I never knew."
In that moment, the world stood still,
A dream so sweet, so full of thrill.
When I awoke, my heart still raced,
The thought of you, my mind embraced.
If only dreams could all come true,
I'd wake to a world where you already knew

8. I Wonder

I wonder if you feel the same,
When you smile, when you say my name.
Do your thoughts ever drift my way,
Like mine do, day after day?

When we talk, do you feel the spark,
That lights up the room, even in the dark?
Do your heartbeats race when we're near,
Or is it just me, holding onto this fear?

I catch your eyes, and for a while,
I wonder if I've seen that smile.
Is it for me, or just the air,
That's filled with something we both share?

I wonder if you think of me,
The way I dream of what could be.
Am I just a thought, or something more,
A feeling you're afraid to explore?

I'm caught between hope and doubt,
A quiet love, I can't let out.

I wonder if you feel the same,
But for now, I'll just whisper your name.

9. In The Quiet Between Us

There's a quiet way you look at me,
Like you're holding a secret, just underneath.
Your smile lingers a little too long,
Like it knows something, but doesn't belong.

You laugh at my jokes, even the small ones,
And when I'm silent, you don't turn and run.
You're always there when I need a friend,
But sometimes I wonder, is it more you intend?

In the little things, I see the clues,
A touch, a glance, a way you choose
To be close when the world feels far,
Like you've noticed me—just who you are.

Your words seem soft, but they carry weight,
Like there's something more that we're meant to create.
I'm not sure yet, but I feel it too,
That maybe, just maybe, you feel it too.

So here we are, in this quiet space,
A subtle hint that we're in the same place.
Not spoken out loud, but understood,
That something more is probably good.

10. The Fragile Line Between Us

I sit with a weight I can't explain,
A mix of hope and quiet pain.
You're my friend, my safe, bright place,
But my heart beats faster when I see your face.

I wonder, if I let you know,
Would you stay, or would you go?
Would the laughter fade, the comfort die,
If you learned the truth I try to hide?

I treasure the bond we've slowly made,
Every joke, every promise laid.
But my feelings grow beyond what's true,
And I'm scared of what I might lose with you.

Could you still smile the way you do,
If you knew my heart belongs to you?
Would the ease between us start to fray,
Or would you gently pull away?

So I keep my love locked deep inside,
Afraid to ruin this perfect tide.
For losing you would break my heart,
And tear this fragile world apart.

11. A Moment Of Vulnerability

The words were there, right on my tongue,
A song unsaid, a song unsung.
I looked at you, my heart was loud,
But fear stood tall, a shadowed cloud.

I almost spoke, I almost tried,
But what if it changed the way you smiled?
What if the bond we've always shared,
Was broken by the love I dared?

So I bit my tongue, I turned away,
And let my chance just slip, decay.
I laughed along, I played it cool,
While my heart burned, a quiet fool.

You didn't see, you'll never know,
The love I hide, the ache I show.
But maybe one day, I'll find the will,
To say the words my heart keeps still.

12. The Language Of Our Eyes

It wasn't a touch, no words were said,
But when our eyes met, my heart was led.
There was something there, a silent spark,
A feeling that lingered, deep in the dark.

Your gaze held mine, steady and true,
Like you were searching for something I knew.
In that quiet moment, I felt the weight,
Of emotions unsaid, of a twist of fate.

There was a softness, a depth in your eyes,
A kind of knowing, no need for disguise.
It wasn't a promise, but it felt the same,
Like you were calling me, but without a name.

In that brief glance, my world stood still,
A thousand things I couldn't yet fill.
Maybe you felt it, maybe you didn't,
But in that moment, hope sparkled, unhidden.

It wasn't much, but it was enough,
A look that said everything without being tough.
And now I wonder, each time we meet,
If your eyes will say what words can't repeat.

13. Reflecting On What-Ifs

What if I told you, just for a day,
What I've been holding, hidden away?
Would the laughter change, would it fade,
Or would we find something new, unafraid?

What if I said, "It's you I see,"
Not just a friend, but something more to me?
Would you smile, would you step closer,
Or would it push us farther from each other?

I wonder what would happen if the truth slipped out,
Would we laugh, would we fight, or be filled with doubt?
Would things stay the same, or would they shift,
Like the tides pulling us, giving us a lift?

What if I took the chance, let go of the fear,
And told you how much I wish you were near?
Would the world change, or would it stand still,
As I waited for you to feel the same, or maybe just feel?

In this moment, I don't know the way,
But I can't help but dream, day after day.
What if you felt it too, what if we could try,
To see where this goes, to just ask why?

But for now, I keep it inside,
Wondering if the "what-ifs" will ever collide.

14. Accepting The Unknown

I don't know what the future holds,
Or if we'll ever be more than this, untold.
Maybe I'll never know what you feel inside,
Maybe I'll just keep these thoughts I can't hide.

But here we are, and that's enough,
The friendship we share, it's real, it's tough.
I've held on to dreams, let them play,
But today, I let the hope just fade away.

I won't ask for more than you can give,
I'll cherish the moments we both live.
Maybe the "what-ifs" will never be real,
But I'll keep the friendship, and that's how I'll heal.

It's okay to wonder, to dream a little bit,
But I won't let it break me, not one bit.
If you never feel the same, that's alright,
I'll hold on to today, and let go of the night.

So here's to the unknown, and to what might be,
To the love I carry, but set free.
Because for now, this is enough,
And in this moment, I'm just grateful for us.

15. A Turning Point

It happened so suddenly, I didn't expect,
A shift in the air, a quiet effect.
You looked at me, and for a beat,
Everything I knew felt incomplete.

You said something small, but it changed the way
I saw you, the words you didn't say.
There was a pause, a flicker of light,
And I knew, somehow, this felt right.

I could feel my heart begin to race,
As I looked for something in your face.
Was it real? Or just a dream?
Could this be more than what it seemed?

I wanted to speak, to ask, to know,
But something held me back, a quiet glow.
You didn't say it, but I could feel,
That something shifted, something real.

In that moment, everything felt new,
Like we'd crossed a line, and we both knew.

Maybe it's the start, or maybe the end,
But right now, we're more than just friends.

I don't know where this road will go,
But in that moment, it felt like hope.
A turning point, a leap of faith,
And I couldn't go back, not to that place.

16. The Question I Can't Answer

The Question I Can't Answer

You ask me again, with that smile in your eyes,
"Who's the one?" like it's no surprise.
I laugh it off, pretend it's just light,
But inside, my heart starts to take flight.

I keep it hidden, my secret untold,
Afraid to show what's been growing so bold.
You ask with patience, a hint of hope,
But I hold back, still learning to cope.

I tell you, "I'll never tell him, not today,"
But I can't hide the words I want to say.
You laugh it off, like it's just a game,
Not knowing you're the one fueling the flame.

You press me again, "Who is he, then?"
And I wish I could say, but I hold it in.
Your curiosity makes me ache,
But I can't risk making my heart break.

So I dodge the question, twist my words tight,
Pretend it's not you, keeping me up at night.
You smile, and I wonder if you already know,
That the one I love is you—though I'll never show.

You keep asking, but I'll never tell,
The secret I keep, the heart I don't sell.
Because some things are too precious to share,
And maybe one day, I'll take the dare.

17. The Fear Of Being Seen

There's a part of me I keep tucked away,
Hidden so deep, I'm afraid it might stray.
It's not just the thoughts that I keep inside,
But the feelings I've learned to carefully hide.

When you look at me, I want to let go,
To show you the things I'm scared you won't know.
But the fear is real, and it holds me tight,
What if you don't see me in that light?

What if the real me isn't enough,
What if I'm too much, or not strong enough?
What if the me that feels all this love,
Is too raw, too honest—something you're not sure of?

So I smile, I laugh, and I stay on the surface,
Not letting you see that behind the perfect,
There's a heart that's fragile, a soul that aches,
And a love that trembles with every breath it takes.

I wonder if you'd still look at me the same,
If I let you in, if I said your name,
And told you the truth of what I'm feeling—
Would you run? Or would you keep on healing?

But the fear keeps me locked, too scared to break,
The chance of losing you feels like too much at stake.
So I hide the real me, keep it unseen,
And wonder if you'd still love me, if you knew what I mean.

18. What Happens After The Hint?

I told myself I wouldn't, but here I am,
Hoping for a sign, a glimpse, or a plan.
You don't know what I'm holding inside,
But I wait, with my heart open wide.

I dropped a hint, just a little taste,
Afraid of the answer, but no time to waste.
And now I wonder, does it show?
Are you thinking what I'm thinking, or is it just me alone?

Your silence speaks louder than you know,
My heart races, unsure where to go.
Should I wait, or should I move?
Will your words confirm, or will they disapprove?

I search your face for any sign,
Trying to read between the lines.
Do you feel it too, or am I just scared?
Is this the moment you'll finally be prepared?

I want to hear you say it, I want to know,
But I'm left here wondering, moving too slow.
The wait is heavy, my patience thin,
Just hoping your reaction will let me in.

But for now, I wait in this limbo space,
With hope in my heart, a smile on my face.
And maybe one day, you'll see it too,
That what I've been waiting for... is you.

19. What If I Ruin Us?

I stood there, caught in a swirl of thoughts,
Wondering if this feeling was worth the cost.
What if I tell you and things go wrong?
What if the friendship we share isn't strong?

What if your smile fades away,
And all I've known is lost in a day?
What if this love, this hope I hold,
Turns into something bitter and cold?

I want to say it, but the fear's too loud,
What if I break the silence we've somehow vowed?
What if I ruin everything, just for a chance,
To see if this feeling could ever advance?

The doubt is heavy, it weighs me down,
I question everything, every word, every sound.
Could this change us? Could we fall apart?
Or will we find a way to restart?

In the quiet moments, I let myself wonder,
But the fear keeps me from taking that plunder.

Maybe I'll never know, and that's okay,
But still, I wonder—what if today?

20. What If We Could Be More?

I can't help but wonder, late at night,
If maybe, just maybe, you'll see me right.
Not just a friend, not just a laugh,
But someone you might want in your life—on your path.

There's this feeling inside, quiet and deep,
A hope I've been holding, a secret I keep.
I see the way you smile, and I wish, just once,
You'd look at me like I'm more than just fun.

I don't say it out loud, don't let it show,
But sometimes I wonder if you already know.
Do you ever look at me and think of us,
Beyond the friendship, beyond the fuss?

Maybe I'm hoping for something too much,
Maybe I'm scared to feel that touch,
But in the quiet of my heart, I can't help but dream,
That one day, we'll be more than what it seems.

It's a small, fragile hope, I'll admit,
But it's there, burning a little bit.
And though I can't say it, I'll keep waiting,
Hoping that one day, you'll start relating.

Because deep down, there's a part of me,
That believes we could be more, if only you'd see.

21. The Uncertainty Of The future

I don't know what comes next, and that scares me,
This feeling of not knowing, a constant mystery.
We're here now, just two hearts in sync,
But what happens when the future starts to blink?

I catch myself wondering if you'll stay,
Or if one day you'll simply walk away.
I can't predict where we'll be in time,
But the thought of losing you still makes me climb.

I'm not ready for the unknown, not yet,
But I can't help the way my heart has set.
What if we grow, or what if we fade?
What if this bond was just a passing shade?

I want to believe in the moments we share,
But deep down, I know life isn't always fair.
Will we stay close, or will we drift apart?
It's the uncertainty that makes it hard to start.

But I hold on, even if I'm unsure,
Because something about us feels so pure.
Maybe the future will bring something more,
Or maybe we'll just be memories to adore.

Either way, I'll cherish what's here,
And let go of the fear that clouds my tear.
Because for now, you're here, and I'm here too,
And that's enough to see me through.

22. What If I Lose You?

What if one day, you're not there?
What if the space between us is too much to bear?
You're my friend, my comfort, my calm,
The one who steadies me when life feels wrong.

But sometimes, this fear grips my chest,
A thought I can't shake, a cruel little test.
What if I lose you to time or chance,
Or to silence that grows from an awkward dance?

I think about us, the moments we share,
The laughter, the comfort, the way you care.
But love—this love—complicates it all,
And I'm scared it might lead to a painful fall.

If I tell you the truth, will you walk away?
Or will things between us start to fray?
I don't want to risk what we have right now,
But keeping it in feels heavy somehow.

So I carry this fear, this ache, this doubt,
Hoping our connection won't ever burn out.

Because losing you isn't something I'd survive,
You're the reason my world feels alive.

I'll hold onto us, whatever this means,
Even if it's not what my heart dreams.
Because losing you would break me in two,
And I'd rather have part of you than none of you.

23. In Your Presence I Find Home

It's not a place, it's not four walls,
It's not the echoes of childhood halls.
Home is the way I feel when you're near,
The calm in my chaos, the end to my fear.

It's the way you laugh, how it lights the room,
The way you lift me from my quiet gloom.
Your voice feels like a familiar song,
A melody that's played all along.

It's not the words you say, it's just your being,
The way you see me without me pleading.
I don't have to hide, don't have to try,
With you, my guard just melts, it flies.

You're steady, constant, a place to land,
Like a lighthouse guiding a ship to sand.
When the world is loud and I feel alone,
You remind me that I've always known—

Home isn't bricks, it's not a street,
It's a heart that knows mine, a soul I meet.
And in your presence, I find my ground,
A peace I thought could never be found.

So stay a little longer, don't let this end,
You're more than my anchor, you're more than my friend.
You're the place I run to, the arms I've roamed,
In you, I've found the meaning of home.

24. When Words Fall Short

There are moments when my heart beats loud,
But the words just get lost in the crowd.
I want to say everything, everything true,
But nothing seems right when I try to tell you.

My feelings are tangled, tied up in knots,
A swirl of emotions, too many thoughts.
I want you to know, to truly see,
How much you mean, how much you've come to be.

But when I open my mouth, nothing comes out,
The words feel too heavy, the silence too loud.
It's like my soul is screaming, but I'm standing still,
Caught between saying too much and saying nothing at all, still.

How do I put into words the way you make me feel?
How do I explain that you make everything real?
That in the quiet moments, in the space between,
You make my world brighter than I've ever seen?

I want to tell you, but the fear holds me back,
What if I stumble? What if I lose track?
So I stay quiet, keeping it inside,
Hoping you see it in the way my eyes hide.

It's the hardest thing, this love unsaid,
A truth locked away, stuck in my head.
But somehow, you still know, don't you?
That my heart speaks louder than my words ever do.

25. The Moment I Almost Let Go

There was a time when I almost turned away,
When the weight of my heart felt too heavy to stay.
I told myself it was better this way,
That maybe it's time for me to walk away.

But every step I took felt like a lie,
And with each breath, I asked myself why.
Why did it feel like I was breaking apart,
When all I wanted was to keep you in my heart?

It's like holding onto something that slips through your hands,
Like trying to hold the ocean with the touch of your hands.
You're not just someone I could forget,
You're a piece of me I can't regret.

So I stood at that edge, staring at the fall,
Wondering if letting go would fix it all.
But deep down, I knew it wasn't true,
That walking away would mean losing you.

And in that moment, I held on tight,
Because the thought of losing you didn't feel right.
So I stayed, despite the pain,
Because letting go would only bring more strain.

Sometimes love feels like a tug-of-war,
A battle between wanting more and wanting to restore.
But in the end, I knew one thing for sure,
That letting go was the hardest choice I could endure.

And so I chose to stay, despite the fear,
Because with you, everything feels more clear.

26. The Struggle To Keep It Together

There are days when my smile feels like a mask,
Like I'm pretending, hiding behind a task.
I laugh, I joke, I play my part,
But inside, my heart's breaking apart.

I try to keep my cool, keep it all inside,
But sometimes, the weight feels too much to hide.
I want to scream, to let it all show,
But I don't want you to see me lose control.

I look at you, and I want to say it all,
But the words get tangled, and I build a wall.
I'm afraid if I speak, if I let it out
That the silence between us will be filled with doubt.

I don't want to burden you with this mess,
I don't want to show you how lost I feel, I confess.
So I keep it together, put on a face,
Hoping you'll never see me in this place.

But inside, I'm unraveling, slowly, piece by piece,
Hoping for some moment, some sense of peace.
I wish I could tell you what I'm going through,
But I'm scared that you'll leave me too.

So I'll keep it together, one day at a time,
Hoping the chaos inside won't show in my rhyme.
But sometimes, it's hard to keep the tears at bay,
When the struggle to hold on is too much to relay.

And yet, I smile and laugh and play along,
Because I don't want to face this all alone.
I'll keep it together for as long as I can,
Hoping that maybe, one day, I'll understand.

27. The Words I Couldn't Say

You asked again, the same old game,
"Who's the one you love? What's his name?"
And I laughed it off, like I always do,
Hiding the truth that it's always been you.

"I'll never confess," I said with a smile,
"Not to him, not now, not ever—meanwhile…"
You shrugged, and your laugh felt forced,
Like you were carrying a weight of your own, of course.

"Yeah, yeah," you said, with a downward gaze,
"I'm not that lucky, not in these ways.
A girl like you would never love me,"
Your voice a whisper, a quiet plea.

"What?" I said, my heart in my throat,
A crack in the armor I barely wrote.
"Why would you say that? Don't you see?
Someone out there loves you, as much as I love… 'him.'"

And there it hung, the words unsaid,
A truth so loud it rang in my head.
Did you hear it? Did you know?
Was the silence enough to let it show?

You smiled, but your eyes told another tale,
A flicker of something—too strong, too frail.
In that moment, the world felt still,
Like the universe bent to my will.
But I stayed quiet, too scared to reveal,
The love I've hidden, the way I feel.
So I let the moment slip away,
Hoping maybe you'd hear what I couldn't say.

28. Is It Him You're Asking For, Or Is It You?

You ask me again, your voice so light,
"Tell him you love him—it feels so right."
But why do you push, why do you care?
Is it curiosity, or is something there?

Your questions linger, they pull at me,
Like you're searching for something I can't let you see.
Do you know the truth that hides in my chest?
Or are you just teasing, like all the rest?

"Why won't you tell him?" you ask once more,
Like my silence is something you can't ignore.
But how can I speak when the words I'd say
Would change everything in the light of day?

Do you feel it too, in the air between?
The way my heart races, the things unseen?
Is this your way of saying you know,
That you're the reason I can't let it show?

Maybe you're scared, just like me,
Afraid of the truth and what it could be.
So you keep asking, hoping I'll break,
Hoping the weight of this love I'll forsake.

But I see your eyes, the way they linger,
Like my silence wraps around your finger.
You're asking me to confess to him,
But is it because you wish you were him?

I won't say it—not yet, not now,
But I wonder if you'd stop me somehow.
Maybe you ask because deep down you see,
The one I love has always been you and me.

29. Through My Eyes Not Yours

You asked me again, with that curious gaze,
"What does he look like?"—a question that sways.
And I smiled, with a warmth in my eyes,
Telling you of the stars that light up his skies.

"He's handsome," I said, "in a way that's rare,
With eyes that pull you in, and a soul laid bare.
His smile, it could stop time, make the world stand still,
And his presence? It's something that gives me a thrill."

You listened, but your eyes stayed unchanged,
You couldn't see what I saw, something strange.
How could you not see the beauty so clear,
The way his laughter fills the air with cheer?

I told you his kindness could move mountains tall,
How his heart holds you up when you start to fall.
But you just nodded, a puzzled smile on your face,
As if you couldn't see what I'd embraced.

And in that moment, I realized something true:
Maybe it's not for you to see him like I do.
Maybe this love, in all its silent grace,
Is something that only my heart can embrace.

So I told you, with a sigh and a smile so bright,
"He's handsome, yes, but it's the way he lights up the night.
You may never see him in the same way I do,
But that's the beauty of love—it's mine, not for you."

30. His Brown Skin

His brown skin, like warm cinnamon toast,
A little bit of magic I love the most.
It's the kind of brown that dances in light,
Like a sunset, soft and bright.

It's the color of chocolate, smooth and sweet,
A perfect shade, no one could beat.
It glows in the morning, like the first ray of sun,
A warmth that makes the whole day fun.

When he smiles, it's like caramel shines,
A glow that rivals the best of vines.
It's rich, it's deep, it's simply divine,
I swear his skin should be a goldmine.

And when the rain falls, it's even more grand,
His brown skin glistens like wet sand.
A sparkle, a shimmer, a touch of grace,
That brings a smile to my face.

Oh, his brown skin, how it makes me giggle,
It's like the sun playing a little jiggle.

If I could, I'd bottle it up, you see,
And share it with the world—just to be free.

But for now, I'll treasure it all on my own,
His brown skin, the beauty I've always known.

31. Smile That Melts Me Like Ice In The Sun

His smile, it starts as a spark, so small,
Like the sun rising, breaking the night's call.
And before I know it, it's filling the sky,
A glow so bright, I can't help but sigh.

It's not just a curve, or a twist of the lips,
It's a story told in a soft, gentle grip.
A warmth that spreads from my head to my toes,
A feeling of love that nobody knows.

When he smiles, the world fades away,
It's like the clouds part and let in the day.
All the worries, all the noise, all the doubt,
They disappear with that smile—there's no way out.

It's the kind of smile that makes my heart race,
A smile that time can never erase.
It's a secret language, an unspoken word,
A feeling that makes everything feel unheard.

I don't know how he does it, how it's so pure,
But when he smiles, I'm caught, I'm sure.
It's like magic, simple and true,
And in that moment, all I see is you.

His smile, it melts me, like ice in the sun,
A feeling so sweet, it can't be undone.
It's the warmth of the world wrapped in one glance,
The kind of smile that makes my heart dance.

32. Moonlight

I call you Moonlight, gentle and true,
A name that seems to fit you through and through.
When you ask me why, I just smile,
Letting the silence linger for a while.

How can I explain what words can't say,
The way you brighten my darkest day?
Like the moon that guards the endless night,
You bring me peace, you make things right.

It's not just your glow or the way you shine,
It's the way you make everything feel fine.
When you're near, the world feels at ease,
Like the calm after a stormy breeze.

You're the moon in the sky so deep,
A light that comforts when I can't sleep.
I don't need to explain, don't need to say,
You're my constant, in every way.

So I call you Moonlight, and it's not just a name,

It's how you've changed me, how you've sparked a flame.
Maybe one day, you'll come to see,
That my Moonlight, it's always been you and me.

PART II

33. 5th August—Midnight Confession

It was 5th August, the clock struck twelve,
A moment where my heart could no longer dwell.
The world was quiet, the air so still,
And I found the courage, against my will.

I opened Instagram, my heart in my hands,
Typing a message only my soul understands.
"You mean the world to me," I began to write,
Every word trembling in the glow of the night.

"I love you unconditionally," I softly confessed,
A love I had carried, long unexpressed.
No expectations, no plea for return,
Just the truth of a heart that forever burns.

It wasn't for answers, not to change your mind,
But to free the weight I'd kept confined.
A love so pure, it asked for no gain,

Just a quiet release from its aching pain.

As the clock struck twelve, it felt so clear,
That 5th August was meant for this, my dear.
Through the screen, I sent all my heart,
Hoping you'd feel what words couldn't start.

And though I knew you might not feel the same,
This wasn't a game, no guilt, no blame.
It was simply my truth, a love unspoken,
Finally freed, my silence broken.

34. The Smile Across The Miles

He called me instantly, his voice so clear,
Saying he was in Nepal, and I could hear,
The smile on his lips, the joy in his tone,
As he teased me gently, making it known.

"Oh Mahnoor," he laughed, "I already knew,"
I felt my cheeks blush, my heart beating too.
Embarrassed, I stammered, "I can't even speak,"
My words tangled up, feeling so weak.

But he kept on laughing, his voice light and free,
"Why are you shy, it's just you and me.
Finally, someone loves me, can't you see?
And she's such a beautiful girl, so wild and free."

My heart fluttered, the world felt so small,
In that moment, his words meant everything at all.
He saw me—truly saw me—through the laughter and cheer,
And in his eyes, I felt something sincere.

I could barely respond, my thoughts too fast,
But his words would linger, forever to last.
A moment of truth, in the quiet of night,
When love was confessed, and everything felt right.

35. Still Blushing Still Smiling

I hung up the call, my heart still racing,
Embarrassed, unsure of what I was facing.
But from the very next day, it started anew,
He sent me pictures, his world in view.

A cup of tea in his hand, warm and serene,
A simple moment, but to me, it felt like a dream.
Another of him driving, the road stretched wide,
As if he was sharing the journey, with me by his side.

I smiled at the pictures, my heart skipping a beat,
But I still felt the blush, my nerves incomplete.
Each video, each image, a silent confession,
Of feelings growing, in sweet progression.

Still embarrassed, but deep inside,
I couldn't wait for the next thing he'd confide.
Each picture, a piece of his day,
A little closer to what we couldn't yet say.

36. What Did You See In Me?

He keeps asking, with laughter so light,
"Mahnoor, how did I ever catch your sight?
You're gorgeous, inside and out, can't you see?
How could someone like you fall for me?"

His voice is a mix of shock and disbelief,
Laughing, yet hiding a hint of relief.
"What did you see?" he says with a grin,
"I'll never understand what you found within."

I wish he could feel what my heart knows,
The way his kindness silently glows.
How his laughter lingers, lighting my day,
How he turns my storms to skies of gray.

It's not just his smile or the way he speaks,
But the calm he brings when my heart feels weak.
He's the warmth in the chill, the peace in the storm,
A rare kind of love, so true, so warm.

Still, he asks, with a laugh in his tone,
As if my love is something unknown.
But if only he saw himself through my eyes,
He'd know he's my moon, my stars, my skies.

37. Everything You Don't See

He keeps asking, with laughter so light,
"Mahnoor, how did I ever catch your sight?
You're gorgeous, inside and out, can't you see?
How could someone like you fall for me?"

His voice is a mix of shock and disbelief,
Laughing, yet hiding a hint of relief.
"What did you see?" he says with a grin,
"I'll never understand what you found within."

I wish he could feel what my heart knows,
The way his kindness silently glows.
How his laughter lingers, lighting my day,
How he turns my storms to skies of gray.

It's not just his smile or the way he speaks,
But the calm he brings when my heart feels weak.
He's the warmth in the chill, the peace in the storm,
A rare kind of love, so true, so warm.

Still, he asks, with a laugh in his tone,
As if my love is something unknown.
But if only he saw himself through my eyes,
He'd know he's my moon, my stars, my skies.

38. Perfect In My Eyes

You speak of flaws, your voice unsure,
Listing things I've never noticed before.
Your brown skin—you think it's not enough,
But to me, it's warmth, both gentle and tough.

You think your voice isn't good enough to hear,
But I'd beg for a whisper, just a second, my dear.
Every word you speak is a melody to me,
A sound I crave, more than you'll ever see.

You doubt your looks, think you don't measure up,
But to me, you're perfect—more than enough.
It's not about beauty in the way you see,
It's your heart, your soul, that captivates me.

You think you're not worthy of someone like me,
But don't you know? You're all I need to see.
Every flaw you mention, every doubt you share,
To me, they're just reasons to love you more, to care.

So when you say you're not good enough, my dear,
Just know in my eyes, you're perfect, so clear.

You're more than enough—your skin, your voice,
The person you are makes my heart rejoice.

39. When Love Has No Reason

He asks me softly, with laughter and care,
"Why do you love me? What did you see there?"
I pause, my heart racing, words out of reach,
Because love like this, no words could teach.

How do I explain what I don't understand,
A love so deep, not built by my hand?
It wasn't his smile, though it makes me glow,
Nor his eyes, though they hold a world I long to know.

It's not the way he stands so tall,
Or how his voice feels like a gentle call.
It's nothing I can point to, nothing I planned,
Maybe it's God who placed love in my hand.

Some say love needs a reason to grow,
But this love of mine—there's no reason to show.
It just is, like the stars in the sky,
A quiet truth I can't deny.

So when he asks, "Why me, of all men?"
I laugh, but my heart whispers again:
"You don't need a reason to love someone true,
Maybe love just knew it was meant to be you."

40. What If He Loves Me Too?

What if his heart feels just like mine,
Racing fast in the same perfect time?
What if his eyes, when they meet my own,
Hold the feelings he's never shown?

What if his smile hides a quiet fear,
Of saying too much when I'm standing near?
What if the way he lingers and stays,
Is his own quiet, wordless way?

I wonder if his thoughts ever drift to me,
Like mine do for him, endlessly.
What if he's waiting, just like I do,
Hoping I'll say, I love you too?

Every glance, every laugh, every brush of his hand,
Feels like a language I don't understand.
But what if it's love, simple and true?
What if he's already in love with me too?

I don't know for sure, but the thought feels bright,
Like a secret hope in the quiet night.
And so I'll hold it close, just in case,
That his heart might already know my place.

41. The Weight Of His Strength

He carries the world upon his back,
Silent, unyielding, he stays on track.
A heart so brave, yet burdened by pain,
A warrior who stands in sunshine and rain.

He hides his struggles behind his smile,
Thinking his worth is measured in trial.
But I see the cracks, the places he bends,
The weight he shoulders, the strength that transcends.

He thinks being strong means standing alone,
That his battles are his, his burdens unknown.
But I wish he'd see, just for a while,
That even the strongest deserve to rest and smile.

He doesn't have to carry it all,
It's okay to stumble, to break, to fall.
For even the moon has shadows to hide,
Yet its glow remains, its beauty amplified.

I love him not for the strength he shows,
But for the heart that quietly knows,
That being strong isn't just what you do,
It's being human, and letting love through.

So I'll stand beside him, through thick and thin,
Reminding him strength isn't always within.
Sometimes it's love that lifts the weight,
And together, we'll face whatever fate.

42. Midnight Surprise

I snapped his laugh when he wasn't looking,
Caught his little moments, like pages I'd be bookmarking.
A picture here, a clip there,
Each one a secret, each one I'd share.

His cousin's snaps, his silly grins,
Saved them all, my heart in spins.
Every second a treasure, every smile so bright,
All stitched together for one perfect night.

Then, the clock started ticking,
Midnight was near, and my heart was quickening.
With a deep breath, I hit 'create',
A little edit—oh, it was fate!

The clock struck twelve, and with a grin,
I sent the video, my love tucked in.
No big reveal, no grand speech,
Just a small act, hoping he'd reach.

In that moment, my nerves took flight,
I sent it, and it felt just right.

No words, no fanfare, just a simple send,
A little gift for him—my love I'd extend.

43. A Birthday Midnight

August 29th, the clock ticks near,
The moment's coming, my heart's full of cheer.
I've made a gift, a video sweet,
For him, the one who makes my heart skip a beat.

As the clock strikes twelve, I take a breath,
Send the edit, hoping it's perfect, no less.
No fanfare, no grand reveal,
Just my heart in pixels, that's the deal.

Then a buzz, his brother's video comes,
Of him, standing, trying not to succumb.
They tease him lightly, a laugh in the air,
His cousin jokes, "I love you, Delshad, with flair!"

He laughs, trying to hide it, just so,
His eyes dancing, but he puts on a show.
"Quiet!" he says, with a playful tone,
"Uncle's sleeping next door, leave me alone!"

I smile to myself, heart skipping,
This moment, his laughter, the joy gripping.

And though I can't hear his voice just yet,
I know he's grinning—our bond, set.

A birthday night, full of love and cheer,
I sent my gift, hoping he'd feel it near.
No need for words, just a simple act,
A little video, and love intact.

44. Endless Hours Of You Listening

It's late, and the world is quiet, still,
I pick up the phone, and time begins to fill.
I start to talk, and you just listen,
Your silence a comfort, my heart starts to glisten.

I tell you about my day, the highs and the lows,
The little details, the moments that glow.
I laugh about things that seem so small,
And in your quiet, you catch it all.

You don't need to say a word, just stay,
And let me ramble, in my own way.
I speak of dreams, of plans for the future,
Of things that feel big, and things that are sutured.

But it's not the words that make me feel seen,
It's your silence, your care, your quiet serene.
You don't interrupt, you don't rush the pace,
You let me spill, in this safe, soft space.

And though I go on, hour after hour,
You listen, you're present, your energy's power.
It's like you're right here, though miles away,
And every word I say, you cherish, you stay.

By the time I'm done, and the call comes to end,
I feel lighter, like a breeze with a friend.
I smile softly, knowing you were there,
In your quiet listening, in the love that you share.
So many nights, just me and my voice,
But with you on the line, I always rejoice.
You don't have to say much, but just being near,
Makes everything better, makes everything clear.

In the silence of the night, you hear me the most,
And in that moment, I feel like I'm close,
To the warmth of your heart, even far away,
And it makes me smile, it makes me stay.

45. The Glance That Held The World

The clock ticked past seven, the air felt warm,
The garden alive with a gentle charm.
I stood amidst the leaves and light,
Thinking of nothing, wrapped in the night.

And then, as if drawn by a force unseen,
My eyes turned to where he'd been.
There he was, sitting in his car,
Not so far, yet feeling like a star.

He held the wheel, but his focus was clear,
He wasn't looking at the road or the gear.
He was bent just slightly, leaning in,
As if to bring me closer to where he'd been.

His eyes—they burned with something deep,
A pull, a spark, a secret to keep.
They weren't just glances; they weren't just looks,
They spoke of stories unwritten in books.

I froze in place, my breath unsure,
His gaze was steady, raw, and pure.
It wasn't a gaze you could look away from,
It wasn't the kind you forget when it's gone.

The world seemed to blur, the moment grew bold,
His intensity warm, but it gave me cold.
I wondered what thoughts ran through his mind,
Was it a question, a wish, a sign?

And in that second, I felt his care,
Though not a single word hung in the air
I felt seen, like I'd never been,
Like he was searching for something within.

The garden remained, but it disappeared,
All I could sense was the way he appeared.
He looked at me as if I was a dream,
As if he'd found his favorite scene.

Even now, it lingers on,
The way his eyes were so headstrong.
In that car, with the wheel in hand,
He spoke a language I didn't understand.

And yet, somehow, it said it all,

Without a whisper, a shout, or a call.
A single glance, but it changed the night,
It lit the garden in a brand-new light.

46. Eyes Full Of Love

The road stretched long, but I barely saw,
Lost in a world where only he and I were at war.
Not with words, not with sound, but a silent dance,
Where I stole glances, hoping for a chance.

He drove with focus, his hands firm and steady,
My heart raced faster than the car; I wasn't ready.
From the backseat, my head tilted to see,
The boy at the wheel, unknowingly pulling me.

His cousin beside him, the night calmly passed,
My mom and sister chatted, but my gaze was steadfast.
Every so often, his eyes found the mirror,
And I'd follow his gaze—closer, clearer.

And there it was, that fleeting connect,
An unspoken bond, subtle yet direct.
I was caught, eyes full of love so true,
And I wondered—what did he feel? Did he know too?

His face unreadable, yet it held something,
A question, a spark, or a silent yearning.

I poured my heart through every look,
Praying he'd read the words I never spoke.
The night fell quiet, and so did my mind,
But his reflection stayed, endlessly kind.
And just a day later, his message arrived,
"Mahnoor, what were you doing? How'd you survive?"

"With eyes full of love?" I dared to confess,
"Yes…" he said, leaving my heart a mess.
"That's what I saw—your gaze so tender,
As if I was your world, your heart's defender."

His words echoed, soft yet profound,
In those moments, I felt love unbound.
The car ride was simple, yet it held our fate,
A story told by eyes, not by debate.

And now, every road reminds me of then,
Of the boy at the wheel, and what could've been.
A love confessed in silence, under moonlit skies,
Told through stolen glances and mirrored eyes.

47. The Night To Remember

It started around eleven, just a normal chat,
Him telling his story, me hanging on to that.
I kept asking questions to keep him on the line,
Dragging the conversation, pretending it was fine.

He didn't know I'd planned every word,
Googled the questions, though it sounds absurd.
I'd even written them down in my notes app,
Just to make sure there were no awkward gaps.

Then, out of nowhere, he burst out laughing loud,
"Wait—did you Google this?" he said, so proud.
My cheeks burned hot, caught red-handed there,
But I faked a laugh, pretending I didn't care.

"No, of course not!" I tried to sound smooth,
"These are in my notes—I swear it's the truth."
"Yeahhh, right," he teased, with sarcasm thick,
"You definitely didn't Google—a classic trick."

And just like that, we both fell into fits,
Laughing at each other, not wanting to quit.
His laugh, a melody, one I'd replay in my mind,
A moment so silly, yet so perfectly kind.

By the time the call to prayer softly broke the night,
We'd talked and laughed until the first morning light.
Though we hung up, my heart was still in a spin,
A memory etched, where his laughter begins.

48. Fractures In Our Midnight Calls

The clock strikes twelve, but the warmth feels lost,
Our words, once gentle, now come at a cost.
Each call begins softly, yet spirals off track,
And ends with silence—no way to go back.

Your voice, once soothing, now cuts me deep,
Leaving me restless, unable to sleep.
I replay the moments, the anger, the pain,
And wonder how love could bear such a strain.

You say I'm distant; I say you don't care,
We hang up, hearts heavy, emotions laid bare.
The quiet that follows feels heavy, immense,
A chasm where laughter once made sense.

Do you feel it too—this fear in the air?
That the threads of us might unravel and tear?
I ask myself, will time heal or betray,
Will the colors of us just wither away?

Yet even through cracks, I'm still holding on,
Praying for hope before love is gone.
Because despite the chaos, despite the ache,
You're still the one my heart cannot forsake.

PART III

49. Was It All In My Head?

I told you I loved you,
With every ounce of courage I had,
And you didn't say it back—
Not in words, not quite.
You just smiled, teased,
Let the silence between us fill in the gaps.

At first, I thought I understood,
Believed in the softness of your actions,
The way you listened, the way you looked at me,
The way you stayed.
But now, I wonder—was I wrong?
Did I read too much into the quiet?

We keep breaking over the smallest things,
Calls ending in heavy pauses,
My voice cracking as I say goodbye,
And yours, unreadable,
As if you're holding back words
I'll never be allowed to hear.

It's all unraveling now, isn't it?
And I'm left holding the frayed threads,
Trying to tie them back together,
Trying to make sense of what we were—
Of what I thought we were.
Did I fall in love with the way you stayed close
Without ever stepping in?
Did I create a story
From the looks you gave
And the spaces you left me to fill?

Was I delusional?
To think love was tucked
In the way you spoke my name,
The way you teased me about silly things,
The way you never said, I love you,
But never said, I don't either.

I'm scared now—
Scared that I imagined it all,
That the moments I cherished
Were just shadows of something I wanted.
And as I hang up the call in frustration,
My heart aches for what's slipping away.

Did I imagine us?

Or are we just losing the pieces
Of something that was never whole?

50. 16th December

It came like a whisper,
Yet it struck like a storm.
Your words, deliberate and heavy,
Cut through the quiet of my heart:
"I don't hate you...
I don't love you either."

How does one breathe after that?
How does a heart keep beating
When it's told it was never truly held?
I replied with trembling hands,
"Yeah, you're right,"
But inside, everything felt wrong.

You spoke of time, Of distance,
Of leaving it all to God.
But the silence that followed
Was already unbearable.
The space between us,
Once filled with laughter and care,
Now felt infinite,
Uncrossable.

You said we needed time,
That distance was the only thing left to give.
And somehow, I understood,
But that understanding didn't make it hurt less.
It just made it sting more,
Like a wound that would never heal.
"Let's maintain distance,"
You said,
And with those words,
You locked the door on something we could've had.
You pulled away,
And with it,
I felt the pieces of my world unravel.
I wanted to run after you,
But my voice was drowned by the weight of what I knew:
You were already gone.

That night,
The night of 16th December,
Became my undoing.
A love I thought was endless
Slipped through my fingers.
And as the clock struck midnight,
It left me in the kind of silence
That only heartbreak knows.

51. From First Love To First Heartbreak

It started like a story you'd read
In a fairytale, so perfectly written,
Your words were like songs in the air,
I could feel them, soft, sweet, and golden.

You told me I was everything,
That nothing would tear us apart,
Your voice, once a soothing balm,
Now echoes in my heart like shards of glass.

At first, you promised me forever,
You said, "If anyone's to leave, it'll be you,"
And I believed every word you spoke,
Like a truth carved in stone, unshakable, true.

We laughed, we talked, we dreamed aloud,
You told me you'd never leave,
But now those words ring hollow,
A distant whisper, a broken plea.

Now your voice, once a warm embrace,
Feels like cold hands, pulling away,
The words that once soothed my soul
Are now blades, tearing me apart.
You called me once, your voice a whisper,
"Yes, you won... I'm leaving you."
It felt like the ground beneath me cracked,
Like everything we built just turned to dust.

The first love
All faded into the ache of goodbye,
And I wonder how love that once felt like home
Can leave you standing, lost, asking why?

I gave you my heart, I gave you my trust,
Believing we'd survive the storm,
But somehow, here we are,
And I'm left with this heartbreak to mourn.

You were my first love,
The one I thought would never fade,
But now you're the first heartbreak
That I can't unmake, can't evade.

How do you move on from someone
Who was your everything, your all,
When the person you once adored

Now makes you feel so small?

It's a journey I didn't expect,
One filled with smiles and tears,
But now I see the truth so clear—
Love can turn to pain, and disappear.

Afterword

As I close this chapter, I hope these words gave a voice to your unspoken feelings, your quiet heartbreaks, and your whispered hopes. May you remember that every ending carries the seed of a new beginning.

www.ingramcontent.com/pod-product-compliance
Lightning Source LLC
La Vergne TN
LVHW041113150826
845673LV00007B/2030
* 9 7 9 8 8 9 6 7 3 0 5 2 1 *